discover countries

New Zealand

Jane Bingham

WAYLAND

Published in paperback in 2014
Copyright Wayland 2014

Wayland
Hachette Children's Books
338 Euston Road
London NW1 3BH

Wayland Australia
Level 17/207 Kent Street,
Sydney, NSW 2000

Concept design: Jason Billin
Editors: Jane Bingham/Steve White-Thomson
Design: 320 Design Ltd
Picture research: Jane Bingham/Alice Harman
Consultant: Elaine Jackson
Proofreader: Alice Harman

Produced for Wayland by
White-Thomson Publishing Ltd

www.wtpub.co.uk
+44 (0)843 2087 460

British Library Cataloguing in Publication Data

Bingham, Jane.
New Zealand. -- (Discover countries)
1. New Zealand -- Juvenile literature.
I. Title II. Series
993'.0412-dc23

ISBN-13: 978 0 7502 8089 1
Printed in China

2 4 6 8 10 9 7 5 3 1

Wayland is a division of Hachette Children's Books
an Hachette UK company
www.hachette.co.uk

All data in this book was researched in 2011
and has been collected from the latest sources available at that time.

Picture credits

1 Shutterstock/Graeme Knox; 3 (top)Dreamstime/Markandcressie; 3 (bottom)Shutterstock/PichuginDimitry; 4 (map) Stefan Chabluk; 5 Shutterstock/adam.golabek; 6 Dreamstime/Bjeayes;7 Shutterstock/BenJeayes; 8 Wikimedia/Andrew Turner; 9 Dreamstime/Dave Greenberg; 10 Shutterstock/Rob Woolley; 11Shutterstock/skphotography; 12 Shutterstock/patrimoniodesigns limited; 13 Alamy/Chad Ehlers; 14 Shutterstock/gmwnz; 15 Shutterstock/RuthBlack; 16 Dreamstime/Nigel Spiers;17(top) Shutterstock/DmitryNaumov; 17 (bottom) Wikimedia/Antilived; 18 (left) Dreamstime/Awcnz62; 18(right) Dreamstime/Markandcressie; 19 Shutterstock/gmwnz; 20 Shutterstock/DmitriOgleznev; 21 (left) Shutterstock/rook76; 21 (right) Shutterstock/Neftali; 22 Shutterstock/PichuginDmitry; 23 Dreamstime/BruceJenkins; 24 Dreamstime/Nigel Spiers; 25 Shutterstock/WoodyAng; 26 Corbis/Tim Clayton; 27 (top)Shutterstock/Graeme Knox; 27 (bottom) Shutterstock/_LeS_; 28 Shutterstock/Hugh Lansdown; 29 Shutterstock/Cameramannz; Cover,Shutterstock/Ruth Black (left)/ Shutterstock/adam.golabek (right).

Contents

Discovering New Zealand

New Zealand is an island nation in the southwest Pacific Ocean. It is one of the world's most remote countries. Apart from a few small islands, its nearest neighbour is Australia, which is over a thousand miles away.

A country made of islands

The nation of New Zealand is made up of more than 100 islands, but most New Zealanders live on just two land masses. The North Island and the South Island are separated by a stretch of water called the Cook Strait. Together they form a long, narrow country that is roughly twice the size of Great Britain.

Māoris and Europeans

The earliest settlers were the Māori people, who set out in canoes across the Pacific Ocean from the Pacific Islands. Māoris began to settle in New Zealand around 1250 CE.

The first European to reach New Zealand was the Dutch explorer, Abel Tasman, in 1642. Settlers from Europe began arriving in the 1790s, and in 1840 the country became a British colony. In 1947 New Zealand joined the British Commonwealth as an independent country that recognized the British monarch as its head of state.

Key
- ■ Capital city
- ● Other towns/cities

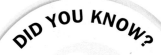
This map shows New Zealand's main cities and major islands.

DID YOU KNOW?

New Zealanders are known all over the world as 'Kiwis'. A kiwi is a small flightless bird that is only found in New Zealand.

New Zealand today

New Zealand's capital is Wellington, but Auckland is its largest city. The country is led by a prime minister, with Queen Elizabeth II as the head of state. The queen is represented in New Zealand by the Governor-General.

New Zealand is a major producer of dairy products, meat, fish, fruit and wine. It is famous for its stunning scenery, which attracts tourists from all over the world.

Today, New Zealand faces some interesting challenges. Exporters have to cope with rising transport costs, and the tourist industry needs to be carefully managed. While New Zealanders welcome growing numbers of visitors, they also have to make sure that their beautiful country stays unspoilt.

▼ New Zealand's capital city, Wellington, is on the southernmost tip of the North Island. Wellington is the country's third largest city, after Auckland and Christchurch.

New Zealand statistics

Area: 267,710 sq km (103,363 sq miles)

Capital city: Wellington

Government type: Parliamentary democracy and a Commonwealth Realm

Bordering countries: None

Currency: New Zealand Dollars (NZD)

Language: English (official) 91.2%, Māori (official) 3.9%, Samoan 2.1%, French 1.3%, Hindi 1.1%, Yue 1.1%, Northern Chinese 1%, other 12.9%.
Note – Language percentages add up to 114.6% because some people registered more than one native language in the 2006 Census.

Landscape and climate

New Zealand is a mountainous country. A line of mountains runs down the centre of the North Island, with low hills on either side. The South Island is dominated by the massive Southern Alps, with hilly farmland to the north and south. The Southern Alps are at their highest in the west, and the flat Canterbury Plains lie to the east.

Glaciers and fjords

On the higher slopes of the Southern Alps, there are more than 300 glaciers (very slow-moving rivers of ice). On the southwest coast of the South Island, steep-sided mountains rise straight out of the sea, and the coastline is broken by fjords (long, narrow coastal valleys with high, rocky sides).

DID YOU KNOW?

Some glaciers are just a few metres long, but the Tasman Glacier, on the South Island, is over 22 km (14 miles) long.

A group of tourists take a guided tour of Fox Glacier on the South Island.

Volcanoes, geysers and earthquakes

New Zealand has at least five active volcanoes, and in the centre of the North Island is Rotorua, a large volcanic plateau with steaming lakes, bubbling mud and spouting geysers (springs of hot water). New Zealand's volcanic action is caused by the movement of two huge tectonic plates (sections of the Earth's crust) beneath the Pacific Ocean. As the plates grind against each other, heat escapes from below the Earth's crust, and results in geysers and other volcanic features.

The movement of the tectonic plates also produces earthquakes. In February 2011 a major earthquake killed 181 people, and destroyed many buildings in the city of Christchurch.

All kinds of weather

Most areas of New Zealand have a mild, temperate climate, but some regions experience more extreme weather. The northern tip of the North Island has a subtropical climate, with hot and damp weather in the summer months. In the snowy heights of the Southern Alps, winter temperatures often drop to minus 10° C.

▶ Some of the geysers at Rotorua can reach a height of 30 m (100 ft).

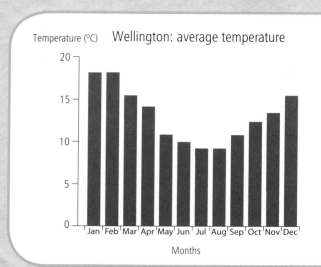

Temperature (°C) Wellington: average temperature

Months

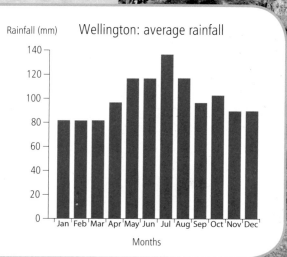

Rainfall (mm) Wellington: average rainfall

Months

7

Population and health

New Zealand is one of the world's most sparsely populated countries. Today, its population is just under 4.5 million (a little more than half the population of New York City). Back in 1950, it was 1.9 million. The country's population has grown extremely fast since the 1950s, due mainly to a sharp rise in the numbers of immigrants. The total number of people living in New Zealand in 2050 is forecast to reach around 5.3 million.

A range of people

There are four main ethnic groups in New Zealand. Over half of all New Zealanders are originally from Europe, while roughly 14 per cent have Māori origins. The other major groups are Pacific peoples and immigrants from Asia. Asian immigrants are New Zealand's fastest-growing ethnic group. Many of them have chosen to move to New Zealand because it offers good opportunities for business and education.

Two languages

New Zealand's first language is English. Its second language is Māori. Less than four per cent of the population speak Māori, but interest in the language is growing. Today, there are two Māori TV channels, and most places have an English and a Māori name.

> ▶ A Māori dancer performing 'haka' – a traditional warrior dance. Māori art and culture play a very important part in the nation's life.

Facts at a glance

Total population: 4,478,548
Life expectancy at birth: 81 years
Children dying before the age of five: 0.6%
Ethnic composition: European 67.6%, Māori 14.6%, Asian 9.2%, Pacific peoples 6.9%, other 12.1%

Age and health

New Zealand today has a fairly young population, with an average age of 36. However, this average is rising, as people live for longer and have fewer children. New Zealand's ageing population may cause serious problems in the future, as the number of people in the workforce shrinks while the need for medical care increases. Heart disease and strokes are the leading causes of death, but the average New Zealander can expect to live to the age of 81. New Zealand has a government-funded health service with free hospital treatment for all.

DID YOU KNOW?
The Māori name for New Zealand is Aotearoa, which means 'land of the long white cloud'.

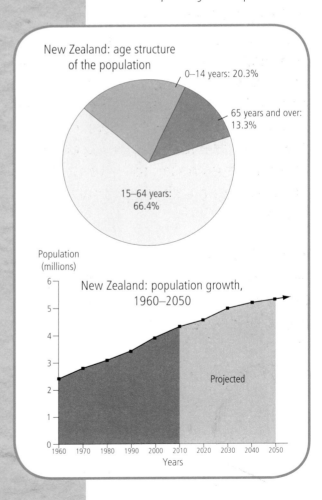

An aerial view of a hospital in a rural area. People in very remote parts of New Zealand are taken to hospital by helicopter.

New Zealand: age structure of the population

0–14 years: 20.3%

65 years and over: 13.3%

15–64 years: 66.4%

Population (millions)

New Zealand: population growth, 1960–2050

Projected

Years

Settlements and living

Most New Zealanders live on just two islands, the North Island and the South Island. The North Island is home to around three quarters of the total population. Almost all the rest of New Zealand's people live on the South Island.

Smaller islands

New Zealand's two main land masses are fringed by many smaller islands. The largest of these is Stewart Island, which lies off the southern tip of the South Island. Stewart Island covers more than 600 square miles, but has fewer than 700 inhabitants. Waiheke Island, near Auckland, is New Zealand's third most populated island, with over 7,000 people (about the same population as a small country town).

A wide-ranging Realm

The Realm of New Zealand is the name given to all the territories (regions and islands) that make up New Zealand. Most of them are ruled directly from New Zealand, but a few have their own governments. Territories with independent governments include a group of South Pacific Islands – the Cook Islands, Niue and Tokelau – and the Ross Dependency in Antarctica. The Ross Dependency is home to two Antarctic research stations. Scott Base is run by scientists from New Zealand and McMurdo Station is an American research centre.

Facts at a glance

Urban population: 86%
(3.7 million)

Rural population: 14%
(0.6 million)

Population of largest city:
1.4 million (Auckland)

Some New Zealanders live in very remote places. This farm cottage is near Arthur's Pass, high in the Southern Alps.

An urban people

Roughly 8 in 10 of all New Zealanders live in urban areas (towns or cities). Most of the population is concentrated in the four major cities of Auckland, Christchurch, Wellington and Hamilton. Of these four cities, Auckland is by far the largest. Almost a third of all New Zealanders live in Auckland and its suburbs.

⬤ Auckland lies on a narrow stretch of land and has two major harbours. It is a lively, multicultural city.

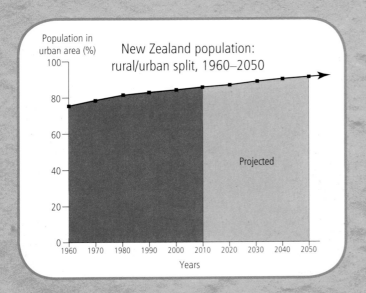

Population in urban area (%)

New Zealand population: rural/urban split, 1960–2050

Projected

Years

DID YOU KNOW?

A sign outside Scott Base in Antarctica reads: 'Welcome to the Capital of the Ross Dependency: Population 85.'

Family life

Patterns of family life are changing in New Zealand. Women are waiting longer than they did in the past to have children. The average age for a woman in New Zealand to have her first child rose from 28 in 2008 to 30 in 2013. Around one in three marriages end in divorce, so it is very common for children to live with just one parent or to grow up in a step-family.

Māori families

In the past, the Māori people of New Zealand lived in large family groups, but this traditional way of life has almost disappeared. Today, most Māoris live in urban areas, and many Māori people have married non-Māoris. Māori family life is similar to that of other New Zealanders, but Māori children usually have more contact with their extended family. It is not unusual for Māori grandparents or uncles and aunts to share the family home.

Facts at a glance

Average children per childbearing woman:
2 children

Average household size:
2.8 people

New Zealanders enjoy the outdoor life. Every year, hundreds of families take part in the Auckland Round the Bays fun walk.

A good place to live

Many New Zealanders enjoy a comfortable lifestyle. The cities and towns are not overcrowded, and there are plenty of green spaces where children can play. In 2013, a United Nations' Human Development Index rated New Zealand as the world's sixth best country to live inThe index was based on life expectancy, education and standard of living.

The great outdoors

For many families, outdoor activities play an important part in their daily lives. Most New Zealanders are less than an hour's drive from the ocean, and no one lives more than four hours away from the mountains. In the warmer months, people enjoy swimming, surfing, cycling, hiking and camping. In winter, skiing and snowboarding are popular activities.

DID YOU KNOW?
Māori friends and family greet each other by pressing their noses and foreheads together so they breathe in each other's breath. This greeting symbolizes the mingling of their spirits.

Religion and beliefs

New Zealand's main religion is Christianity. Just over half of all New Zealanders describe themselves as Christians, although less than 15 per cent are regular churchgoers. In recent years, immigrants from Asia have brought their religions to New Zealand. There are growing numbers of followers of Hinduism, Buddhism, Islam and Sikhism.

Christmas Kiwi-style

New Zealanders of all faiths celebrate Christmas, and most big towns have a Santa parade. Some New Zealanders cook a traditional Christmas lunch with roast turkey, but most people prefer to have a barbecue on Christmas day.

Māori beliefs

The Māori people keep their ancient beliefs alive through stories, dances and ceremonies. Traditional Māori stories describe how the world was created by the marriage of the Sky Father and the Earth Mother, and the birth of their six powerful sons. One Māori legend tells how an ancestor called Maui caught the North Island on the end of his fishing line. This legend explains why the island is shaped like a fish.

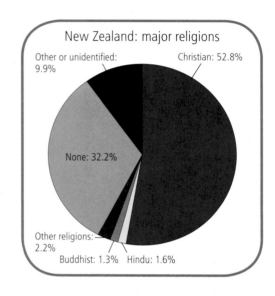

New Zealand: major religions

- Christian: 52.8%
- None: 32.2%
- Other or unidentified: 9.9%
- Other religions: 2.2%
- Buddhist: 1.3%
- Hindu: 1.6%

🔻 There are growing numbers of Hindus in New Zealand. These dancers are taking part in the Hindu festival of Diwali, which is celebrated in Auckland every year.

◀ This Māori carving shows a man with a full facial tattoo, called a moko.

Traditional tattoos

In traditional Māori society, all men had a set of tattoos, known as a moko. Boys were given their first tattoos in a ceremony to mark their coming of age, and later designs were added at important stages of their lives. The face was the main area for tattoos, and a man's moko showed his family history and position in society.

Women outlined their lips and nostrils and had small patterns on their chins. Some men also had swirling double spirals tattooed on their buttocks and thighs. Today, many Māori people choose to have a traditional moko as a way of connecting with their ancient culture.

DID YOU KNOW?
Māori people fly hand-made kites to celebrate the start of their New Year. According to Māori beliefs, the kites create a link between the heavens and the earth.

Education and learning

All children in New Zealand go to school, except for a tiny proportion (about two per cent) who are taught at home. The state provides free education for pupils between the ages of 5 and 18. Over 90 per cent of children in New Zealand attend state schools or schools that are partly funded by the government.

School and beyond

Most state schools are day schools but a few take boarders. The boarders usually come from remote rural areas or have parents who work abroad. Three in ten teenagers leave school when they reach 16, but the rest stay on until they are 18.

New Zealand has eight universities, and many other colleges of further education. These study centres attract students from all over the world. New Zealanders can also enrol on apprentice schemes to learn a skilled job. The schemes cover a wide range of skills including plumbing, electronics, building, furniture-making and boatbuilding.

Facts at a glance

Children in primary school:
Male 99%, Female 99%

Children in secondary school:
Male 95%, Female 97%

Literacy rate (over 15 years):
99%

Many schools in Christchurch were damaged by the earthquake of 2011, and some pupils had to share another school's buildings.

Otago University in Dunedin was founded in 1869. It has a world-class reputation for medical research.

A different way of learning

Many Māori children experience difficulties in school. To help solve this problem, more than 80 wānanga colleges have been set up in New Zealand. In wānanga colleges, teachers stress the importance of passing on traditional knowledge from one generation to the next. They teach Māori culture and performing arts, and also run courses on business, computing, social work and teaching. Wānanga colleges are open to all New Zealanders but they are especially designed for Māori students.

DID YOU KNOW?

Many New Zealand schools teach a game call touch. Touch is played by both boys and girls and is similar to rugby, but much less dangerous.

Māori students learn how to carve traditional sculptures in a wānanga college.

Employment and economy

The job market in New Zealand has changed dramatically over the past 60 years. In the 1950s most people worked in agriculture. Now, roughly three quarters of the country's work force are employed by the government or by other service providers, such as computer businesses. The recent boom in overseas visitors has led to one in ten New Zealanders being employed in tourist-related work.

Jobs for New Zealanders

In the past, New Zealand had an outstanding record of employment, with a very small proportion of its population out of work.

Facts at a glance

Contributions to GDP:
agriculture: 4.7%
industry: 24.3%
services: 71%
Labour force:
agriculture: 7%
industry: 19%
services: 74%
Female labour force:
46% of total
Unemployment rate:
6.4%

New Zealand's economy is no longer dominated by farming. Today, only seven per cent of the population work in agriculture.

During the grape harvesting season, pickers are in great demand.

However, unemployment rose sharply following the global financial crisis of 2008. In mid 2011, roughly six out of every hundred New Zealanders could not find a suitable job, but the employment situation is slowly improving.

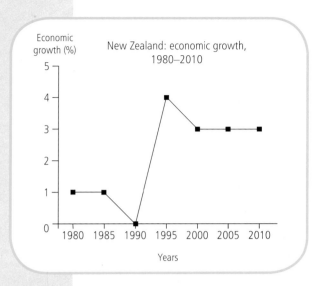

New Zealand: economic growth, 1980–2010

Natural resources

Farming, fishing and forestry have always played an important part in the economy of New Zealand, while wine production is a new area of growth. The country also has some valuable mineral resources, including iron-ore and small deposits of gold. New Zealand makes use of its natural resources to produce energy. Around ten per cent of the country's energy is geothermal (produced by volcanic heat). Another 55 per cent is generated from water that flows through hydroelectric dams.

The fishing industry

New Zealand's fishing industry is big business, with over 90 species of fish and seafood being exported. Sole, snapper and mullet are caught in the shallow waters around the coast, while tuna and shark are fished by deep-water trawlers. Mussels, oysters and salmon are reared in specially managed aquaculture farms. The fishing industry provides valuable jobs for people living in remote coastal areas.

DID YOU KNOW? The Māoris have practised aquaculture for centuries. Māori people living by the coast placed large rocks in the water to make an enclosed area where oysters could breed.

▶ Small boats are used for coastal fishing. This traditional fishing boat is moored at Riverton, on the southern tip of the South Island.

Industry and trade

Food and farm products play a very important part in New Zealand's economy. The country is a major exporter of wool, meat, fish, dairy produce, fruit and vegetables. Manufacturing is not so well-developed, so New Zealanders have to import most of their machinery and equipment, along with vehicles and aircraft, electronics, textiles and plastics.

Trading partners

Until the 1970s, New Zealand sold most of its goods to Britain, but in 1973 Britain joined the European Economic Community (EEC) and ended its special relationship with New Zealand. Britain's move forced New Zealand to find new countries to trade with. Today, New Zealand's main trading partners are Australia, China and the USA.

▼ A salt production plant on the South Island. The plant extracts salt from sea water.

Commemorative stamps were issued between 2001 and 2004 to celebrate the filming of the *Lord of the Rings* trilogy.

DID YOU KNOW?
New Zealand's film studios are based in Wellington, on the North Island. They have been nicknamed 'Wellywood', a name that combines Wellington and Hollywood.

Filmed in New Zealand

New Zealand has a range of manufacturing industries, but the big success story of the last ten years is its film industry. Between 2001 and 2003, director Peter Jackson filmed his *Lord of the Rings* trilogy in New Zealand, and in 2011 he returned to film *The Hobbit*. The state-of-the-art technology used in Jackson's films has proved that New Zealand can compete with studios anywhere in the world. Today, New Zealand is one of the world leaders in special effects and animation.

Made in New Zealand

Most of New Zealand's manufacturing industries rely on the country's natural resources. The country has a large number of food processing and packaging plants. Textile factories produce carpets and fabrics using local wool, and timber mills create wood and paper products. New Zealand also has some metal processing plants, such as New Zealand Steel, which uses locally sourced iron and coal to manufacture steel for use at home and abroad.

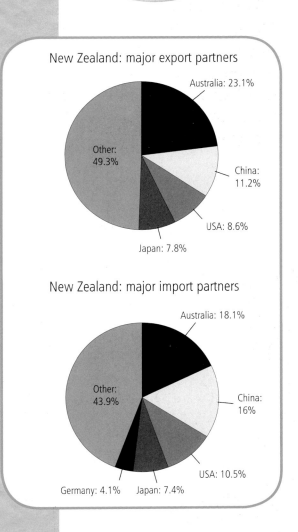

New Zealand: major export partners
- Australia: 23.1%
- China: 11.2%
- USA: 8.6%
- Japan: 7.8%
- Other: 49.3%

New Zealand: major import partners
- Australia: 18.1%
- China: 16%
- USA: 10.5%
- Japan: 7.4%
- Germany: 4.1%
- Other: 43.9%

Farming and food

New Zealand is home to many kinds of agriculture. Farmers raise sheep, cows, pigs and chickens. Goats are kept for their cheese and mohair wool, and deer are reared for their meat (called venison). New Zealand has many arable farms where crops like wheat and oats are grown, and an increasing number of farmers grow fruit and vegetables.

Sheep and cows

New Zealand's sheep farmers produce some of the world's best lamb, and sheep's wool is also an important export. Sheep are generally kept in dry, hilly areas, while dairy farms are found in the wetter regions. New Zealand is famous for its butter, which is especially creamy because its cows feed on very rich grass. As well as producing a range of dairy products, farmers also raise cows to produce beef.

Facts at a glance

Farmland: 2% of total land area

Main agricultural exports: dried milk, lamb, kiwi fruit, beef, butter

Main agricultural imports: palm nuts, wheat, raw sugar, sorghum, soy beans

Average daily calorie intake: 3,130 calories

Sheep rearing is still an important part of the country's economy, but in the 1980s dairy farming took over as New Zealand's highest-earning farming industry.

Fruit growers

New Zealand has an ideal climate for growing apples and pears. Apple growers produce a wide range of varieties for export, but Gala and Braeburn are especially popular. Peaches and plums are mainly consumed in New Zealand, while apricots and cherries are mostly exported. The kiwi fruit is New Zealand's major fruit export, and the country has more than 2,000 kiwi fruit growers.

New Zealand wine

Winemaking is one of New Zealand's great success stories. Over the past ten years, the number of wineries has almost doubled, and New Zealand now has more than 600 wine producers. New Zealand's wine producers make red and white wine, but they are famous for their outstanding white wines. The finest wine comes the Marlborough region, on the northern tip of the South Island, and the Hawke's Bay area, on the eastern coast of the North Island.

⬤ Apple picking in an orchard near Hawke's Bay on the North Island. Hawke's Bay is New Zealand's leading area for apples and peaches.

DID YOU KNOW?
New Zealand's beekeepers produce very high-quality honey. They also breed bees for export. Approximately 20 tonnes of packaged bees are exported live each year.

Transport and communications

Travelling around New Zealand is a challenge. With its high mountains, long stretches of coastline and many islands, it is not an easy country in which to move around. Fortunately, however, there is a good network of roads. New Zealanders rely heavily on their cars, and most of the government transport budget is spent on roads, rather than on buses and trains.

From tracks to roads

Most of the country's roads follow the routes of the ancient Māori walking tracks. Later settlers built roads to take their sheep to market. The country's main route is State Highway 1. It runs from the northern tip of the North Island to the southern tip of the South Island, with a car ferry link between the two islands.

▼ New Zealand's export trade relies on container ships. All heavy goods are transported by sea, and some food is exported in refrigerated ships.

Ships, planes and trains

Shipping is very important for New Zealand. Container ships are used for exporting and importing goods, while coastal ships are useful for transport around the country. Regular ferries run between the North and the South Islands, and there are ferry services to the major offshore islands.

Most people and many goods arrive in New Zealand by air, and planes are often used to transport people to other islands. Trains carry some heavy goods across the country. There are three long-distance passenger services, and urban rail services operate in Wellington and Auckland.

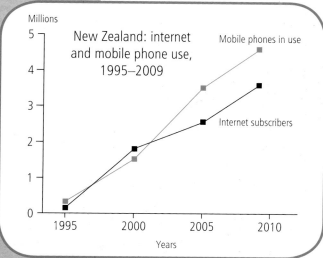

⬤ Sea planes take visitors to remote areas. This plane is landing on Lake Taupo, in the North Island's volcanic region.

A well-connected nation

Perhaps because their country is so isolated, New Zealanders like to stay in touch. In 2013, 83 per cent of all New Zealanders had access to the internet. Facebook and and Twitter are widely used by the younger generation. After the Christchurch earthquake in June 2011, people used social networks to share their photos and

DID YOU KNOW?

New Zealanders are keen phone users. A recent survey showed that there are more mobile phones than people in New Zealand!

Millions

New Zealand: internet and mobile phone use, 1995–2009

Mobile phones in use

Internet subscribers

Years

Leisure and tourism

New Zealand offers great opportunities for fun and leisure. Most New Zealanders take their holidays at home, and growing numbers of tourists visit each year. Tourist numbers have risen steadily since 2000, reaching a total of over 2.5 million in 2010. New Zealanders have responded to the rise in tourism by opening new restaurants and hotels, and developing outdoor leisure resorts.

Facts at a glance

Tourist arrivals
2000: 1,780,000
2005: 2,353,000
2010: 2,501,000

A passion for sport

Most New Zealanders love sport. Cricket, tennis, golf and soccer are all very popular, but the national passion is rugby. The New Zealand All Blacks are the world's top-ranking rugby team. In 2011, 60,000 spectators gathered in Auckland to watch the final of the Rugby World Cup, in which the All Blacks narrowly beat France.

The whistle's gone, and the All Blacks celebrate a hard-fought 9-8 victory over France in the 2011 Rugby World Cup Final at Eden Park, Auckland.

Tourist attractions

One of the main attractions of New Zealand is its scenery. Both the North and the South Islands have sandy beaches, rolling hills, forests and snow-capped mountains. At the northern tip of the North Island is Abel Tasman National Park, with its tropical rainforest. The Tongariro National Park, in the heart of the North Island, has three active volcanoes. Milford Sound, on the southwest coast of the South Island, is part of the spectacular Fiordland National Park. The Sound has been described as one of the wonders of the world.

Fine food

New Zealand's restaurants have a reputation for excellent food made from fresh ingredients. Specialities include local lamb, beef and venison, and a range of delicious seafood, including mussels, crayfish and oysters. A popular New Zealand vegetable is kumara, a kind of sweet potato. New Zealand's best-known dessert is the pavlova, a large meringue case filled with fruit and cream.

⊙ Tourists come from all over the world to marvel at the scenery in Milford Sound.

DID YOU KNOW?
The first commercial bungee jump was set up in Queenstown, on the South Island, in 1988. Queenstown is still one of the world's most popular centres for bungee jumping.

⊙ Green-lipped mussels are a speciality of New Zealand.

Environment and wildlife

The natural environment of New Zealand is unlike that of any other country. This is because the islands of New Zealand split off from other parts of the world between 130 and 85 million years ago. Very gradually, a set of unique plants and creatures evolved in this isolated land.

Land of birds

When the Māoris arrived around 1250 CE, the only mammals that existed on New Zealand were a few species (types) of bat. Instead, there were many types of birds, reptiles and insects. The birds included several flightless species, such as the large Moa. The Moa were easy prey for hunters and soon became extinct.

Today, many species of New Zealand's birds are in danger of dying out, but people are making great efforts to preserve their wildlife. The New Zealand Conservation Trust runs schemes to protect the nesting areas of endangered birds.

Facts at a glance
Proportion of area protected: 24.4%
Biodiversity (known species): 2,861 species
Threatened species: 112

▶ The takahē is a flightless bird that lives in the mountains of the South Island. Today, the takahē is an endangered species, with only about 200 birds surviving.

The tuatara is only found in New Zealand. The name tuatara comes from the Māori language and means 'peaks on the back'.

Ancient forests

New Zealand has some very unusual reptiles and plants. In the northern part of the North Island, there are forests of kauri trees. These giant trees grow up to 50 m (164 ft) tall and have trunks that can measure up to 4 m (13 ft) thick. Kauri trees have changed very little since the Jurassic period.

An environment under threat

Records show that average temperatures in New Zealand are rising. At the same time, sea levels are creeping upwards and glaciers are shrinking. New Zealand's government has a policy of cutting down emissions of carbon dioxide gas in an attempt to slow down climate change.

DID YOU KNOW?

The tuatara has a 'third eye' on the top of its head that is sensitive to light. Scientists think the eye may help it to judge the time of day or the season.

Glossary

animation the process of creating a moving film by filming a series of drawings one after the other

aquaculture rearing of fish and seafood in contained areas of water

arable growing crops, such as wheat or corn

colony a country that has been settled in by people from another country, and is controlled by the settlers' country

commemorative in memory of something or someone

Commonwealth Realm a group of territories that all have the British monarch as their head of state

culture the way of life and traditions of a particular group of people

emission production or output

ethnic groups groups of people who belong to different races

evolve to change very gradually over millions of years

export to sell goods or services to another country

generate to make or create (electricity)

geothermal energy energy that comes from volcanic heat under the ground

geyser spring of hot water that shoots up suddenly from the earth

glacier large, slow-moving river of ice, formed by many layers of snow

head of state someone who is recognized as the overall ruler of a country, but who does not have the job of ruling the country from day to day

hydroelectric dam a dam where pressure from fast-flowing water is changed into electricity

immigrant someone from abroad who comes to live permanently in a country

import to buy goods or services from another country

inhabitants people who live in a certain place

life expectancy the length of time a person can expect to live

mineral resources metals and other substances that are found in the earth

mohair fine, long wool that comes from Angora goats

monarch king or queen

multicultural made up of people from many different countries

natural resources plants, soil, water and metals that are found naturally in an area

offshore in the sea, away from the main shore

parliamentary democracy a county that is governed by a parliament, whose members have been voted for in a general election

plateau wide area of flat land high up in hills or mountains

prime minister the leader of a government

resort place where people go to enjoy themselves

rural to do with the countryside or agriculture

stroke sudden damage to the brain that causes part of the body to become stiff and paralysed

sub-tropical lying just below or just above the regions of the Earth known as the tropics. A subtropical climate is hot and steamy for part of the year

temperate neither very hot nor very cold

trilogy set of three

unique unlike anything else

United Nations Human Development Index a measurement of whether a country is a good place to live. The index is run by the United Nations, an organization that works for peace, human dignity and well-being.

urban to do with towns or cities, and town or city life

wānanga college a college where Māori culture is taught

Topic web

Use this topic web to explore themes related to New Zealand in different areas of your curriculum.

Maths
New Zealand's currency is the New Zealand dollar (NZD). Find out how many New Zealand dollars there are in £1. Use the internet to discover the cost of a meal in a restaurant in New Zealand. Convert this cost into pounds.

Citizenship
New Zealand was the first country in the world to grant women the right to vote in elections. When did women gain this right in New Zealand? When did they gain it in the UK and the USA? Make a list of reasons why women should have the right to vote.

History
When explorers from Europe first reached New Zealand, the Māori people tried to drive them away. Find out about the dramatic history of New Zealand in the 1600s and 1700s.

Science
New Zealand is a region of volcanic activity. Find out what causes volcanoes to erupt. Draw a cutaway labelled diagram of an erupting volcano.

New Zealand

English
Using reference books, tourist brochures and the internet, plan and write a programme for an exciting ten-day family holiday in New Zealand.

Design and Technology
Use the Internet to research Māori bird kites. Then type 'Māori bird kite lesson plan' into an internet search engine to find instructions for making a simple kite, using newspaper, string and light wooden rods.

Geography
Around 200 million years ago, New Zealand was part of a giant southern continent called Gondwana. Then it very gradually drifted away from other areas of land. Use reference books and the internet to find out about Gondwana, and how Australia and New Zealand were formed.

ICT
Use the internet to plan a journey through New Zealand using three or more types of public transport. Your journey should start at Whangarei on the North Island and end at Invercargill on the South Island. Work out how long the journey will take and write a journey timetable.

Further information and index

Further reading

DK Eyewitness Travel Guide: New Zealand (Dorling Kindersley, 2010)
The Māori of New Zealand (First Peoples), Steve Theunissen (Lerner Publishing Group, 2003)
The Way Out Bunch – Discovering Endangered Animals: Who Lives in New Zealand? Jenny Tulip and Dawn Smith (RoperPenberthy, 2009)

Web

www.kids.nationalgeographic.com/kids/places/find/new-zealand
Facts and photos about New Zealand from National Geographic Magazine
www.kidskonnect.com/subject-index/26-countriesplaces/325-new-zealand.html
Fast facts and lots of links to websites about New Zealand
www.doc.govt.nz/conservation/native-animals
An introduction to New Zealand's animals and birds
www.history-nz.org/index.html
A site on New Zealand's history, including a timeline and sections on Māori culture, legends and games

Index